TIKTOK MARKETING UNVEILED:

A Comprehensive Guide for Business Owners

Description: Unlock the full potential of TikTok for your business with this comprehensive and accessible eBook, designed exclusively for business owners like you. From beginners to advanced users, our 25 conversational chapters will help you harness the power of TikTok marketing to build your business, improve revenue, and sell more products. Say goodbye to jargon and confusion and start your TikTok journey with confidence.

Table of Contents:

Chapter 1: Introduction to TikTok Marketing

- TikTok's role in modern business marketing.
- Why TikTok is relevant for your business.
- The potential impact on revenue and product sales.

Chapter 2: Setting the Stage

- Step-by-step guide to creating a TikTok Business Account.
- Navigating the TikTok App, including key features and settings.

Chapter 3: Your Brand Story

- Crafting a compelling brand narrative that resonates with TikTok users.
- Emphasizing authenticity and relatability in your storytelling.

Chapter 4: Identifying Your Target Audience

- Strategies to pinpoint your ideal TikTok viewers.
- Tailoring your content to appeal to your target demographic.

Chapter 5: Content Creation 101

- Tips and techniques for creating engaging TikTok content.
- Understanding video formats, transitions, and effects.

Chapter 6: Going Viral on TikTok

- Proven strategies to increase the reach and engagement of your TikTok videos.
- Leveraging trends and timing for maximum impact.

Chapter 7: Leveraging Trends and Challenges

- Exploring the world of TikTok trends and challenges.
- How to participate effectively while staying true to your brand.

Chapter 8: Hashtags and Captions

- The role of hashtags and captions in TikTok success.
- Crafting attention-grabbing captions and selecting the right hashtags.

Chapter 9: Engaging with Your Audience

- Building meaningful connections with your TikTok viewers.
- Responding to comments and fostering a community.

Chapter 10: Collaborations and Partnerships

- Strategies for growing your business through collaborations with other TikTok users.
- How to identify and approach potential partners.

Chapter 11: Analysing TikTok Analytics

- Understanding TikTok's built-in analytics tools.
- Using data to refine your TikTok marketing strategy.

Chapter 12: TikTok Advertising

- A comprehensive guide to TikTok advertising options, including sponsored content and paid campaigns.
- Budgeting and optimizing your ad spend.

Chapter 13: TikTok Challenges and Contests

- Running successful TikTok challenges and contests to engage your audience.
- Examples of effective TikTok campaigns.

Chapter 14: Handling Negative Feedback

- Strategies for managing criticism and turning it into an opportunity for growth.
- Maintaining a positive brand image.

Chapter 15: Cross-Promotion with Other Platforms

- Integrating TikTok with your existing social media and marketing efforts.
- Tips for seamless cross-promotion.

Chapter 16: TikTok for E-Commerce

- Selling products effectively on TikTok, including product demos and user-generated content.
- Strategies for driving sales through TikTok.

Chapter 17: Legal Considerations

- Navigating potential legal issues on TikTok, such as copyright and privacy concerns.
- Protecting your business from legal pitfalls.

Chapter 18: Financial Strategies

- Budgeting and financial management for TikTok marketing campaigns.
- Measuring the ROI of your TikTok efforts.

Chapter 19: Beating the Competition

- Strategies for outshining your competitors on TikTok.
- Identifying and capitalizing on your unique selling points.

Chapter 20: Pricing Strategies

- Determining the right pricing strategy for your products on TikTok.
- Factors to consider when setting prices.

Chapter 21: Time Management

- Practical tips for finding the time to manage your TikTok marketing efforts.
- Efficient content creation and scheduling.

Chapter 22: Building a Website for Your Business

- Simplified steps to create a website for your business, including hosting and design options.
- Integrating your TikTok content into your website.

Chapter 23: Achieving Self-Sufficiency

- Balancing the responsibilities of being a business owner and maintaining a presence on TikTok.
- Strategies for achieving self-sufficiency in your business.

Chapter 24: Your Business Legacy

- Preparing for long-term success and sustainability on TikTok.
- Strategies for building a lasting brand presence.

Chapter 25: Conclusion and Next Steps

- Summarizing key takeaways from the book.
- Encouragement and guidance on taking your TikTok marketing to the next level.

Disclaimer: This eBook is intended for informational purposes only and should not be considered as professional advice. The author and publisher are not responsible for any outcomes resulting from the implementation of the strategies and tips presented in this eBook. It is advisable to consult with a professional for specific business and legal advice.

With "TikTok Marketing Unveiled," you'll gain the confidence and knowledge needed to thrive on TikTok while keeping your hard work, self-sufficiency, and family in mind. Start building your business and achieving your revenue goals today!

CHAPTER 1:
INTRODUCTION TO
TIKTOK MARKETING

Welcome to the exciting world of TikTok marketing, where creativity knows no bounds, and your business can reach millions of potential customers in just a matter of seconds. In this chapter, we'll embark on a journey to understand how TikTok can be a game-changer for your business, whether you're a seasoned entrepreneur or just starting out. We'll explore why TikTok is relevant, its potential impact on your revenue, and how it aligns with your goal of providing for your family and contributing to society.

Why TikTok Matters for Your Business

TikTok is not just another social media platform; it's a cultural phenomenon. With over a billion monthly active users worldwide, TikTok has emerged as a powerful marketing tool for businesses of all sizes. But why should you care?

Firstly, TikTok offers an unparalleled opportunity to connect with a diverse and engaged audience. Unlike some other platforms, TikTok's algorithm values creativity and discovery. This means that even small businesses can quickly gain attention and traction if they produce compelling content.

Secondly, TikTok's user base spans different age groups, making it a versatile platform for reaching both younger and older demographics. No matter your target audience, there's a good chance they're scrolling through TikTok.

The Potential Impact on Revenue and Product Sales

At the heart of every business owner's goals are revenue growth and increased product sales. TikTok can be a powerful catalyst for achieving these objectives.

- **Boosting Brand Visibility:** By creating engaging and shareable content, you can increase brand awareness and visibility, putting your business on the radar of potential customers.
- **Driving Traffic:** TikTok can be an effective tool for driving traffic to your website, online store, or other digital platforms, ultimately leading to more sales opportunities.
- **Conversion Opportunities:** TikTok's interactive features and creative storytelling allow you to connect with your audience on a deeper level. This connection can lead to increased conversions and customer loyalty.
- **Product Showcases:** TikTok provides an ideal platform for showcasing your products or services. You can demonstrate how your offerings solve problems, meet needs, or simply make people's lives better.

Aligning with Your World View and Goals

As a business owner, your world view likely centres around hard work, self-sufficiency, taking care of your family, and contributing to society. TikTok marketing aligns with these values in several ways:

- **Hard Work:** Building a successful presence on TikTok requires dedication and effort, values that resonate with your work ethic.
- **Self-Sufficiency:** TikTok offers a level playing field for businesses, where success is not determined solely by budget but by creativity and authenticity.
- **Family Support:** TikTok can be a platform where you showcase your family's involvement in your business, creating a personal connection with your audience.

- **Contribution to Society:** TikTok provides an avenue to share your business's positive impact on society, aligning with your desire to contribute positively.

In this eBook, we will guide you through every aspect of TikTok marketing, from setting up your business account to running successful ad campaigns. Whether you're a TikTok novice or have some experience, we've got you covered. By the end of this journey, you'll have the knowledge and confidence to leverage TikTok's potential and drive your business towards success.

So, are you ready to unlock the potential of TikTok and take your business to new heights? Let's get started!

CHAPTER 2: SETTING THE STAGE

Welcome to Chapter 2 of "TikTok Marketing Unveiled." In this chapter, we'll walk you through the essential steps of setting up your TikTok Business Account and getting familiar with the TikTok app. We understand that some business owners may be completely new to TikTok, so we'll keep it simple and easy to follow.

Creating Your TikTok Business Account

If you haven't already done so, it's time to create your TikTok Business Account. Here's how:

- **Download the TikTok App**: Visit your device's app store (App Store for iOS or Google Play Store for Android) and search for "TikTok." Download and install the app.
- **Open TikTok**: Once installed, open the TikTok app by tapping its icon. You'll be greeted with a captivating video feed of various TikTok content.
- **Sign Up or Log In**: If you already have a personal TikTok account, you can convert it into a Business Account. If not, tap "Sign Up" to create a new account. You can use your email, phone number, or social media accounts to register.
- **Select a Username**: Choose a username that represents your business. Keep it simple and easy to remember. Remember, your username is how people will find and identify you on TikTok.
- **Complete Your Profile**: Add a profile picture that

features your business logo or a relevant image. Write a brief, engaging bio that tells viewers what your business is all about. Include any essential contact information, such as your website or email address.

- **Convert to a Business Account**: If you started with a personal account, you can convert it to a Business Account in your settings. This gives you access to additional tools and analytics.

Getting to Know the TikTok App

TikTok's interface is user-friendly, but let's go over the basics:

- **Home Feed**: The Home feed is where you'll see a continuous stream of TikTok videos. Swipe up to scroll through the content.
- **Discover Page**: This icon, usually represented by a magnifying glass, takes you to the Discover page, where you can explore trending challenges, content, and hashtags.
- **Recording Button**: Tap the plus (+) sign at the bottom centre to record your TikTok video. You can record by holding down the button or by using the timer.
- **Sound Selection**: Choose a background sound or music for your video by tapping the music note icon. You can search for songs, use popular tracks, or browse TikTok's library.
- **Effects and Filters**: On the right side of the recording screen, you'll find options for adding effects, filters, and text to your video. Get creative and experiment with these features.
- **Video Duration**: TikTok videos can be up to 3 minutes long, but shorter videos (15-60 seconds) are often more engaging.
- **Editing Tools**: After recording, you can trim, cut, and edit your video within the app. Take your time to perfect your content.

- **Captions and Hashtags**: Add a catchy caption and relevant hashtags to your video to increase its discoverability.
- **Posting and Engagement**: Once your video is ready, tap the checkmark to proceed. You can add captions, tags, and choose your audience. Interact with viewers by responding to comments and engaging with other content.

Congratulations! You've now successfully set up your TikTok Business Account and have a basic understanding of the app's interface. In the upcoming chapters, we'll delve deeper into TikTok marketing strategies and how to create compelling content that resonates with your audience. Stay tuned, and let's continue our TikTok marketing journey together!

CHAPTER 3: YOUR BRAND STORY

In the world of TikTok marketing, storytelling is your superpower. It's how you connect with your audience on a personal level, evoke emotions, and leave a lasting impression. In this chapter, we'll explore the art of crafting your brand story for TikTok, a story that will resonate with your viewers and build a strong, loyal following.

Why Your Brand Story Matters

Imagine TikTok as a giant storytelling platform where millions of stories are shared daily. To stand out, you need a compelling and authentic brand story that captures the essence of your business. Here's why it matters:

- **Human Connection**: A well-told story humanises your business. It allows viewers to relate to you, your values, and your mission. People don't just buy products or services; they buy into the story behind them.
- **Emotional Engagement**: Emotions drive actions. A powerful brand story can evoke emotions that motivate viewers to engage with your content, follow your account, and become customers.
- **Memorability**: A memorable story is more likely to be shared and talked about. It helps you leave a lasting mark in viewers' minds.

Crafting Your Brand Story

Now, let's break down the process of crafting your brand story:

- **Know Your Why**: Start by asking yourself why you started your business in the first place. What problem were you trying to solve? What passion or mission drives you? Your "why" is the heart of your story.
- **Your Unique Selling Proposition (USP)**: What makes your business unique? Identify what sets you apart from the competition. It could be your product, your values, your customer service, or a combination of factors.
- **Customer-Centric Approach**: Your story should focus on how your business benefits your customers. Highlight the positive impact your products or services have on their lives.
- **The Hero's Journey**: The hero's journey is a classic storytelling structure. Cast yourself and your business as the hero, overcoming challenges and obstacles to provide a solution to your customers' needs.
- **Authenticity**: Authenticity is key on TikTok. Be yourself and let your personality shine through. Authenticity builds trust, and trust leads to loyal customers.
- **Visual Storytelling**: TikTok is a visual platform. Use imagery, videos, and animations to complement your narrative. Show, don't just tell.
- **Consistency**: Your brand story should be consistent across all your TikTok content. This creates a cohesive brand identity that viewers can easily recognise.

Elements of a Great Brand Story

A great brand story typically includes the following elements:

- **Introduction**: Who you are, what your business is about, and your mission or values.
- **Conflict**: The challenges or problems your business addresses.
- **Resolution**: How your products or services provide solutions or benefits.

- **Characters**: You, your team, and satisfied customers can all be characters in your story.
- **Emotion**: Infuse your story with emotion. Whether it's joy, humour, inspiration, or empathy, emotions make stories memorable.

Sharing Your Brand Story on TikTok

Now that you have a compelling brand story, it's time to share it with your TikTok audience:

- **Video Series**: Consider breaking your story into a series of shorter videos. This keeps viewers engaged and encourages them to follow along.
- **Use Relevant Hashtags**: Include relevant and trending hashtags to increase the discoverability of your story.
- **Engage with Comments**: Respond to comments on your videos, fostering a sense of community and connection.
- **Collaborate**: Collaborate with other TikTok users to introduce your brand story to new audiences.
- **Analytics**: Monitor the performance of your storytelling videos through TikTok's analytics to understand what resonates with your viewers.

Your brand story is a powerful tool for connecting with your audience and differentiating your business on TikTok. In the following chapters, we'll explore how to tailor your storytelling to appeal to your target audience and create content that leaves a lasting impact.

CHAPTER 4: IDENTIFYING YOUR TARGET AUDIENCE

Welcome to Chapter 4 of "TikTok Marketing Unveiled." In this chapter, we will delve into the crucial aspect of identifying your target audience on TikTok. Understanding your audience is the foundation for creating content that resonates and drives results for your business.

Why Identifying Your Target Audience Matters

Identifying your target audience is not just a marketing buzzword; it's a strategic necessity. Here's why it matters:

- **Relevance**: Knowing your audience enables you to create content that speaks directly to their interests, needs, and desires. This relevance grabs their attention.
- **Engagement**: Engaged viewers are more likely to interact with your content, follow your account, and become loyal customers. Identifying your audience helps you foster this engagement.
- **Efficiency**: Targeted content saves time and resources. You can avoid creating content that doesn't resonate with your core audience, ensuring a higher return on investment.
- **Conversion**: When your content aligns with your audience's preferences, you increase the chances of turning viewers into paying customers.

Steps to Identify Your Target Audience

Now, let's explore the steps to identify your target audience on TikTok:

1. Market Research: Begin by conducting market research to gain insights into your industry, niche, and competition. Analyse your competitors' audiences to understand who they are reaching.

2. Define Demographics:

- **Age**: Determine the age group your products or services appeal to.
- **Gender**: Identify if your audience is predominantly male, female, or balanced.
- **Location**: Consider the geographic locations where your audience is concentrated.

3. Psychographics:

- **Interests**: Explore the hobbies, interests, and passions of your potential customers.
- **Lifestyle**: Understand their lifestyle choices, values, and aspirations.
- **Challenges**: Identify the problems or challenges they face that your business can solve.

4. Behaviour:

- **Online Behaviour**: Learn about their online behaviour, such as social media usage and platforms they frequent.
- **Purchase Behaviour**: Analyse their buying habits and decision-making process.

5. Customer Personas: Create customer personas based on the data you've gathered. These personas are fictional representations of your ideal customers and help you humanise and understand your audience better.

6. Survey Your Existing Customers: If you have an existing customer base, survey them to gather insights about their preferences and what attracted them to your business.

7. Analyse TikTok Audiences: Utilize TikTok's built-in analytics to gain insights into the demographics and interests of your current TikTok followers. This data can provide valuable information about your existing audience.

8. Competitor Analysis: Examine the TikTok accounts of your competitors or businesses in a similar niche. Observe the demographics and engagement levels of their followers.

9. Test and Refine: As you start creating TikTok content, pay attention to who engages the most with your videos. Use this data to refine your understanding of your target audience over time.

Creating Content for Your Target Audience

Once you have a clear understanding of your target audience, it's time to create content tailored to their preferences:

- **Content Themes**: Develop content themes that resonate with your audience's interests. For example, if you sell outdoor gear, create content around camping, hiking, and adventure.
- **Tone and Style**: Adjust your content's tone and style to match the preferences of your audience. If your audience is youthful, use a more casual tone; if it's more professional, maintain a polished style.
- **Use Relevant Hashtags**: Incorporate popular and relevant hashtags that your target audience follows. This increases the discoverability of your content.
- **Engage and Interact**: Actively engage with comments and messages from your audience. Respond to questions, acknowledge feedback, and build a sense of community.
- **Consistency**: Consistently create and post content to keep your audience engaged and returning for more.

Understanding your target audience is an ongoing process. As your business evolves and TikTok trends change, your audience's preferences may shift. Stay adaptable and keep refining your understanding to maintain a strong connection with your viewers. In the upcoming chapters, we'll explore how to create content that captivates and resonates with your target audience on TikTok.

CHAPTER 5: CONTENT CREATION 101

Welcome to Chapter 5 of "TikTok Marketing Unveiled." In this chapter, we'll delve into the fundamentals of creating engaging TikTok content that captures the attention of your target audience. Whether you're a beginner or looking to enhance your content creation skills, you'll find valuable insights and tips here.

Understanding TikTok's Unique Appeal

Before we dive into the nitty-gritty of content creation, it's crucial to understand what makes TikTok unique and why it has become such a sensation:

- **Short-Form Video**: TikTok videos are short, typically ranging from 15 to 60 seconds. This brevity keeps viewers engaged and encourages them to consume more content in a shorter time.
- **Vertical Video**: TikTok is designed for vertical video, making it easily viewable on mobile devices. This format maximizes screen space and provides an immersive viewing experience.
- **Sound and Music**: TikTok offers an extensive library of music and sounds that users can incorporate into their videos. Music plays a significant role in setting the mood and making content more enjoyable.
- **Engagement Features**: TikTok's interactive features, like duets, challenges, and reactions, encourage viewers to participate and engage with content creators.

Now, let's explore the steps to create compelling TikTok content:

STEP 1: DEFINE YOUR CONTENT GOALS

Before you start filming, it's essential to define your content goals. Ask yourself:

- What do you want to achieve with this video?
- Are you looking to entertain, educate, inspire, or promote a product?
- What action do you want your viewers to take after watching?

Clarity on your goals will guide your content creation process.

STEP 2: PLAN YOUR CONTENT

While TikTok encourages spontaneous and authentic content, some planning can go a long way:

- **Storyboard**: Outline the main scenes or shots you want to include in your video.
- **Script or Outline**: Prepare a rough script or key points you want to cover in your video.
- **Props and Outfits**: Gather any props or choose outfits that align with your video's theme.

STEP 3: CAPTIVATING INTRO

The first few seconds of your video are crucial in grabbing viewers' attention. Consider:

- An intriguing hook or question.
- Quick and attention-grabbing visuals.
- Engaging music or sound.

STEP 4: KEEP IT CONCISE

TikTok videos are short, so every second counts. Get to the point quickly and maintain a brisk pace throughout your video.

STEP 5: VISUAL STORYTELLING

TikTok is a visual platform, so focus on:

- Clear and appealing visuals.
- Use of gestures, expressions, and body language to convey your message.
- Visual storytelling techniques like transitions and overlays.

STEP 6: MUSIC AND SOUND

Selecting the right music or sound is vital. Ensure it complements your content, sets the mood, and adds to the overall experience.

STEP 7: ENGAGE YOUR AUDIENCE

Encourage interaction with your content:

- Use text overlays to pose questions or prompts.
- Ask for comments, likes, shares, or follows.
- Participate in challenges or trends relevant to your niche.

STEP 8: EDIT AND ENHANCE

TikTok provides built-in editing tools. Use them to:

- Trim and cut clips.
- Add effects, filters, and stickers.
- Adjust video speed.

STEP 9: THUMBNAIL AND CAPTIONS

Create an eye-catching thumbnail that represents your video. Write captions that provide context, include relevant hashtags, and encourage engagement.

STEP 10: TEST AND ITERATE

Don't be afraid to experiment and learn from your audience's response. Analyse your video's performance through TikTok's analytics and adjust your content strategy accordingly.

Conclusion

Creating engaging TikTok content is both an art and a science. While there are guidelines to follow, creativity and authenticity are your greatest assets. As you continue on your TikTok marketing journey, remember that practice makes perfect. With each video you create, you'll refine your skills and better understand what resonates with your audience. In the following chapters, we'll explore specific content strategies and tactics to help you achieve your marketing goals on TikTok.

CHAPTER 6: GOING VIRAL ON TIKTOK

Welcome to Chapter 6 of "TikTok Marketing Unveiled." In this chapter, we'll explore strategies and tips to help your TikTok content go viral. Going viral on TikTok can significantly expand your reach, increase engagement, and boost brand awareness. Let's dive in.

Understanding TikTok Virality

Going viral on TikTok means that your content resonates with a vast audience and spreads rapidly. TikTok's algorithm plays a significant role in determining which videos go viral. Here's how it works:

- **The "For You" Page (FYP)**: TikTok's FYP is a feed of curated content tailored to each user. It's where users discover new content and trends. When your video lands on a user's FYP, it has the potential to go viral.
- **Engagement Metrics**: TikTok's algorithm considers various factors, including likes, comments, shares, and the amount of time users spend watching your video. High engagement signals that your content is valuable and engaging.
- **Consistency**: Consistently creating and posting quality content increases your chances of having videos featured on the FYP.

Strategies for TikTok Virality

Now, let's explore strategies to increase your chances of going viral on TikTok:

1. Trend Participation

- Keep an eye on trending challenges and hashtags. Participating in these trends can expose your content to a wider audience.
- Put your unique spin on trends. Add your personality and creativity to stand out from the crowd.

2. High-Quality Production

- Invest in good lighting, clear audio, and stable camera work. Quality matters on TikTok.
- Use TikTok's built-in editing tools to enhance your video. Experiment with effects, transitions, and filters to make your content visually appealing.

3. Timing is Key

- Post your content when your target audience is most active. TikTok analytics can provide insights into your audience's online behaviour.
- Consider the time zone of your target audience if you have an international following.

4. Captivating Opening

- Hook viewers within the first few seconds of your video. An intriguing start can encourage viewers to keep watching.
- Use text overlays or captions to pose questions or create curiosity.

5. Audience Interaction

- Encourage comments, likes, shares, and follows by asking viewers to engage with your content.

- Respond to comments promptly to foster a sense of community.

6. Engage with Trends

- Create content around current events, holidays, or relevant pop culture trends.
- Use trending sounds and music in your videos to tap into the latest trends.

7. Storytelling

- Craft compelling narratives in your videos. Tell stories that resonate with your audience emotionally.
- Use the power of storytelling to draw viewers in and keep them engaged until the end.

8. Consistency

- Post regularly and consistently. Building an active presence on TikTok requires ongoing effort.
- Create content that aligns with your niche or industry, so viewers know what to expect from your account.

9. Collaboration

- Collaborate with other TikTok users, especially those with larger followings. Cross-promotion can introduce your content to new audiences.

10. Experiment and Learn

- Don't be afraid to experiment with different content styles, formats, and niches.
- Analyse TikTok's analytics to understand what works best for your audience and adjust your strategy accordingly.

Conclusion

Going viral on TikTok is an exciting and attainable goal with the right strategies and creativity. Keep in mind that virality isn't guaranteed, but by consistently creating high-quality, engaging content and participating in trends, you can increase your chances of capturing the attention of TikTok's vast and diverse user base. In the next chapters, we'll explore more advanced TikTok marketing techniques to further enhance your success on the platform.

CHAPTER 7:
LEVERAGING TRENDS
AND CHALLENGES

Welcome to Chapter 7 of "TikTok Marketing Unveiled." In this chapter, we'll delve into the world of TikTok trends and challenges, and how you can effectively leverage them to enhance your marketing efforts. TikTok is known for its trends, and participating in them can significantly boost your visibility and engagement.

Understanding TikTok Trends and Challenges

TikTok trends and challenges are popular themes, dance routines, music tracks, or concepts that gain rapid popularity and traction within the TikTok community. They often involve users creating their own content based on a specific trend or challenge.

Here's why understanding and leveraging these trends and challenges matter:

- **Increased Visibility**: Participating in trending challenges or using trending music can get your content featured on the "For You" page, significantly increasing your reach.
- **Community Engagement**: Joining a trend or challenge allows you to connect with a broader community of TikTok users who share similar interests.
- **Creative Inspiration**: Trends and challenges can provide inspiration for creating new and exciting content, helping you stay relevant and engaging.

How to Leverage TikTok Trends and Challenges

Now, let's explore how you can effectively leverage TikTok trends and challenges for your marketing:

1. Stay Informed

- Regularly explore TikTok's "Discover" page and browse through trending hashtags and challenges. This will help you stay up-to-date with the latest trends.
- Follow popular creators in your niche to see what trends they're participating in.

2. Choose Relevant Trends

- Not every trend or challenge will be relevant to your business or brand. Select those that align with your industry, products, or target audience.
- Consider trends that allow you to incorporate your brand or products naturally.

3. Add Your Unique Twist

- While it's important to follow the core elements of a trend or challenge, add your unique twist to make your content stand out.
- Show your brand's personality and style within the context of the trend.

4. Use Trending Music

- Incorporate popular and trending music into your videos. TikTok's music library is extensive, so you're likely to find tracks that fit your content.
- Music adds a dynamic element to your videos and can evoke emotions that resonate with viewers.

5. Engage Authentically

- Participate in trends and challenges authentically. Be genuine and enthusiastic about the content you're creating.

- Interact with others who are also engaging in the same trends. Collaboration can further boost your reach.

6. Timing is Crucial

- Jump on trends and challenges while they are still gaining momentum. The earlier you participate, the higher the chances of your content getting noticed.
- Keep an eye on emerging trends and be quick to adapt your content strategy.

7. Measure Results

- Monitor the performance of your content that leverages trends and challenges. Pay attention to engagement metrics, such as likes, comments, shares, and follows.
- Use TikTok's analytics to understand which trends are driving the most success for your business.

8. Stay Consistent

- While trends are constantly evolving, consistency in your content creation and posting schedule is key to building a strong TikTok presence.
- Blend trend participation with your regular content strategy to maintain a cohesive brand identity.

Conclusion

Leveraging TikTok trends and challenges can breathe new life into your marketing efforts on the platform. It's an effective way to connect with a wider audience, showcase your brand's creativity, and ride the wave of TikTok's ever-changing landscape.

Remember that trends come and go, so it's essential to adapt and experiment with different approaches. In the following chapters, we'll explore more TikTok marketing strategies to further enhance your presence on this dynamic platform.

CHAPTER 8: ENGAGING WITH YOUR AUDIENCE

Welcome to Chapter 8 of "TikTok Marketing Unveiled." In this chapter, we'll explore the art of engaging with your TikTok audience. Building a strong, interactive community is essential for the success of your TikTok marketing efforts. Let's dive into strategies and tips for meaningful engagement.

The Power of Audience Engagement

Audience engagement is the heart of TikTok marketing. When you engage with your audience effectively, you:

- **Foster Loyalty**: Engaged viewers are more likely to become loyal followers and customers.
- **Boost Visibility**: TikTok's algorithm rewards content that receives high engagement, increasing your chances of appearing on the "For You" page.
- **Build Relationships**: Engagement allows you to build genuine relationships with your audience, leading to trust and brand advocacy.

Strategies for Audience Engagement

Here are effective strategies for engaging with your TikTok audience:

1. Respond to Comments

- Take the time to respond to comments on your videos. Acknowledge compliments, answer questions, and engage in meaningful conversations.
- Responding promptly shows that you value your

audience's input.

2. Ask Questions

- Encourage audience participation by asking questions in your videos or captions. Pose questions that spark curiosity or require viewers to share their opinions.
- Use text overlays to display questions or prompts within your videos.

3. Host Q&A Sessions

- Host regular Q&A sessions where you answer questions from your audience. This can be a live video or a series of video responses.
- Collect questions from your audience beforehand to ensure you cover topics of interest.

4. Run Contests and Challenges

- Organize contests or challenges that require viewers to participate. This can include creating content related to your brand or products.
- Provide clear instructions and offer prizes or recognition for the best entries.

5. Collaborate with Your Audience

- Collaborate with your audience by featuring their content in your videos or giving shoutouts to active followers.
- Recognize and celebrate your audience's creativity and contributions.

6. Conduct Polls and Surveys

- Use TikTok's interactive features like polls to gather opinions or preferences from your audience.

- Share the results and insights from polls, showing that you value their input.

7. Behind-the-Scenes Content

- Offer a glimpse behind the scenes of your business or content creation process. This can create a sense of exclusivity and connect viewers to your brand on a personal level.
- Share challenges, triumphs, and lessons learned along the way.

8. Showcase User-Generated Content

- Showcase content created by your audience that features your products or services. This not only demonstrates user satisfaction but also encourages others to create their own content.
- Always seek permission and give proper credit when using user-generated content.

9. Stay Positive and Supportive

- Maintain a positive and supportive tone in your interactions with the audience. Encourage kindness and respectful conversations within your community.
- Address criticism or negative feedback gracefully and constructively.

10. Analyse and Adapt

- Use TikTok's analytics to track engagement metrics and understand which types of content and interactions resonate the most with your audience.
- Adjust your content strategy based on audience preferences and feedback.

Conclusion

Audience engagement on TikTok is a dynamic and ongoing process that requires time and effort. However, the rewards in terms of brand loyalty, increased visibility, and genuine connections are well worth it. As you continue to engage with your TikTok audience, remember that authenticity, empathy, and responsiveness are key to building a thriving community on this vibrant platform.

In the following chapters, we'll explore advanced TikTok marketing techniques and strategies to further elevate your brand's presence and impact on TikTok.

CHAPTER 9: CRAFTING COMPELLING CALLS TO ACTION (CTAS)

Welcome to Chapter 9 of "TikTok Marketing Unveiled." In this chapter, we'll explore the importance of crafting compelling Calls to Action (CTAs) in your TikTok marketing strategy. CTAs are the guiding force that encourages your audience to take specific actions, and they play a crucial role in achieving your marketing goals.

Understanding the Role of CTAs

Calls to Action (CTAs) are directives that prompt your audience to take a specific action after interacting with your TikTok content. Whether you want them to like, share, comment, visit your website, or make a purchase, CTAs guide your viewers toward meaningful engagement.

Here's why CTAs are essential in TikTok marketing:

- **Clarity**: CTAs provide clear instructions to your audience, reducing any ambiguity about what you want them to do next.
- **Engagement**: Well-crafted CTAs can boost engagement metrics such as likes, comments, shares, and follows.
- **Conversion**: CTAs can be instrumental in converting viewers into customers by directing them to your website or product pages.
- **Audience Interaction**: Encouraging interactions like comments can spark conversations and community

building around your content.

Effective CTA Strategies

Now, let's explore strategies for creating compelling and effective CTAs on TikTok:

1. Be Specific

- Clearly state the action you want your audience to take. Use concise language that leaves no room for confusion.
- For example, instead of a vague CTA like "Check it out," opt for "Swipe up to visit our website for more details."

2. Create a Sense of Urgency

- Use words that convey urgency to motivate immediate action. Phrases like "limited time offer," "act now," or "don't miss out" can instil a sense of urgency.

3. Offer Value

- Explain the benefits of taking the desired action. Let your audience know what's in it for them.
- For instance, if you want viewers to subscribe to your channel, you can say, "Subscribe for weekly tips and exclusive content."

4. Use Visual Cues

- Incorporate visual elements such as arrows, pointing fingers, or animated overlays that guide viewers' attention to the CTA.
- These cues draw the eye and reinforce the desired action.

5. Leverage Text Overlays

- Add text overlays within your video to reinforce your CTA visually. These can be subtitles or captions that emphasize the action you want viewers to take.

- Use contrasting colours to make the text stand out.

6. Incorporate Sound

- Audio cues can be effective in drawing attention to your CTA. Consider using a sound effect or a change in music to coincide with the CTA.
- Keep in mind that many viewers watch TikToks with the **sound off**, so make sure your visual cues are strong enough to convey the message independently.

7. Interactive CTAs

- Encourage viewers to participate actively. Ask questions, run polls, or host interactive challenges that require engagement.
- For example, "Comment your favourite emoji, if you love this product!"

8. Test and Iterate

- Don't be afraid to experiment with different CTAs to see which ones resonate best with your audience.
- Analyse the performance of your videos to understand which CTAs lead to the desired actions.

Conclusion

Effective Calls to Action (CTAs) are integral to your TikTok marketing strategy. They guide your audience toward specific actions that align with your business objectives. Whether you aim to boost engagement, drive website traffic, or encourage product purchases, well-crafted CTAs can be a powerful tool in achieving your goals.

As you continue to create TikTok content, keep refining your CTA strategies to maximize audience engagement and conversion rates. In the upcoming chapters, we'll delve into more advanced TikTok marketing techniques to further elevate your success on the platform.

CHAPTER 10: MONETISING YOUR TIKTOK PRESENCE

Welcome to Chapter 10 of "TikTok Marketing Unveiled." In this chapter, we'll explore how to monetize your TikTok presence effectively. While TikTok is primarily a platform for creative expression and community-building, there are opportunities to generate income and turn your passion into a source of revenue.

The TikTok Monetisation Landscape

TikTok offers various avenues for monetization, and understanding these options can help you leverage your presence on the platform to its fullest potential. Here are some key monetisation methods:

1. Brand Partnerships and Sponsorships

- Collaborate with brands that align with your content and audience. Brands often pay TikTok creators to promote their products or services.
- Ensure that partnerships are authentic and resonate with your followers to maintain trust.

2. Affiliate Marketing

- Promote products or services from brands and earn a commission for every sale generated through your unique affiliate link.
- Choose products or services that genuinely interest your audience to increase conversion rates.

3. Selling Merchandise

- If you have a dedicated fan base, consider designing and selling merchandise related to your content or brand.
- Use TikTok to showcase your merchandise and provide links to purchase.

4. Live Streaming Gifts and Donations

- TikTok allows viewers to send virtual gifts during live streams. Creators receive a portion of the revenue generated from these gifts.
- Engage with your audience during live streams and offer exclusive content to incentivize donations.

5. TikTok Creator Fund

- Once you meet specific eligibility criteria, you can join the TikTok Creator Fund, which allows you to earn money based on the number of views your videos receive.
- Keep in mind that the Creator Fund's earnings may vary, and it's important to consistently produce engaging content.

6. Selling Digital Products

- If you have valuable knowledge or digital products to offer, such as e-books, courses, or presets, promote and sell them to your TikTok audience.
- Use your TikTok content to demonstrate the value of your digital products.

7. Crowdfunding and Patreon

- Platforms like Patreon enable you to create a

subscription-based community where your most dedicated fans can support you in exchange for exclusive content, perks, and interactions.

- Promote your Patreon or crowdfunding campaign on TikTok to attract supporters.

8. Direct Advertisements

- Reach out to businesses and negotiate direct advertising deals, especially if your niche aligns with their target audience.
- Create engaging and authentic advertisements that resonate with your followers.

Effective Strategies for Monetisation

To effectively monetize your TikTok presence, consider these strategies:

1. Build a Strong Brand

- Develop a clear and authentic personal brand that resonates with your audience. Consistency in content and messaging is key.

2. Focus on Engagement

- Prioritise building a loyal and engaged following. Engage with your audience through comments, responses, and live streams.

3. Diversify Income Streams

- Explore multiple monetization options to reduce dependence on a single source of income. Diversification can provide stability.

4. Stay Authentic

- Maintain the authenticity that attracted your audience in the first place. Overly promotional content can turn viewers away.

5. Track Your Performance

- Regularly analyse your TikTok analytics to understand which content performs best and which monetization methods yield the highest returns.

Conclusion

Monetising your TikTok presence can be a rewarding endeavour, allowing you to turn your passion and creativity into a source of income. However, success in TikTok monetisation requires dedication, a deep understanding of your audience, and a commitment to delivering valuable content.

As you explore the various monetisation methods available on TikTok, remember that building trust with your audience should always be your top priority. In the following chapters, we'll delve into advanced TikTok marketing techniques to help you further optimise your strategy and achieve your goals on the platform.

CHAPTER 11: ADVANCED TIKTOK ADVERTISING STRATEGIES

Welcome to Chapter 11 of "TikTok Marketing Unveiled." In this chapter, we'll dive into advanced TikTok advertising strategies that can help you elevate your marketing efforts on the platform. TikTok offers a range of advertising options designed to reach your target audience effectively.

Understanding TikTok Advertising

TikTok advertising allows businesses to promote their products or services to a vast and engaged audience. Before diving into advanced strategies, let's briefly review the primary types of TikTok ads:

- **In-Feed Ads**: These are short video ads that appear in users' "For You" feed as they scroll through TikTok. They can be up to 60 seconds long and include a clickable link.
- **Branded Hashtag Challenges**: Brands create unique challenges, encourage user participation, and promote them using a sponsored hashtag. This can lead to viral engagement.
- **Branded Effects**: Brands can create customized augmented reality (AR) effects and filters for users to use in their videos. These effects promote brand recognition.

- **TopView Ads**: These are in-feed ads but have the added benefit of being the first thing users see when they open the TikTok app. They offer maximum visibility.
- **Branded Content**: Collaborate with popular TikTok creators to promote your products or services authentically. Creators can produce engaging content that resonates with their followers.

Advanced Advertising Strategies

Now, let's explore advanced TikTok advertising strategies to maximize the impact of your campaigns:

1. Audience Segmentation

- Utilise TikTok's advanced targeting options to segment your audience based on demographics, interests, behaviour, and device type.
- Tailor your ad content to each audience segment to increase relevancy and engagement.

2. A/B Testing

- Experiment with different ad creatives, headlines, and call-to-actions. A/B testing allows you to identify the most effective elements of your ads.
- Analyse the performance of each variant and allocate your budget to the most successful versions.

3. Storytelling

- Craft compelling and concise narratives within your ad content. Storytelling can captivate the audience and make your brand message memorable.
- Ensure that your ad delivers a clear and emotionally resonant message.

4. Influencer Collaborations

- Partner with influencers who align with your brand's values and target audience. Influencers can create authentic content that connects with their followers.
- Leverage the influencer's expertise in creating engaging TikTok content.

5. User-Generated Content

- Encourage users to create content related to your brand or products. User-generated content can generate buzz and increase trust.
- Highlight the best user-generated content in your advertising campaigns.

6. Data-Driven Decisions

- Continuously monitor the performance of your TikTok ads using the platform's analytics. Pay attention to key metrics such as click-through rate (CTR) and conversion rate.
- Use data insights to make informed decisions and optimize your ad campaigns.

7. Interactive Elements

- Incorporate interactive elements within your ads to engage viewers. Encourage viewers to swipe, tap, or engage with AR effects.
- Interactive ads are more likely to capture and maintain users' attention.

8. Remarketing Campaigns

- Implement remarketing campaigns to re-engage users who have previously interacted with your brand or website.
- Target users who have shown interest but haven't converted yet.

9. Seasonal Promotions

- Align your TikTok advertising campaigns with seasonal events, holidays, or special promotions. Seasonal content can resonate well with viewers.
- Plan ahead and create timely ad campaigns that capture the spirit of the season.

10. Cross-Promotion

- Promote your TikTok ads on other social media platforms and your website to maximise reach.
- Cross-promotion can help drive traffic to your TikTok profile and boost engagement.

Conclusion

Advanced TikTok advertising strategies can elevate your brand's presence and impact on the platform. By harnessing the power of TikTok's advertising options and implementing these advanced techniques, you can effectively reach and engage your target audience, drive conversions, and achieve your marketing goals.

As you navigate the world of TikTok advertising, remember to stay creative, data-driven, and adaptable. In the following chapters, we'll continue to explore advanced marketing tactics and trends to keep you at the forefront of TikTok marketing.

CHAPTER 12: MEASURING TIKTOK MARKETING SUCCESS

Welcome to Chapter 12 of "TikTok Marketing Unveiled." In this chapter, we'll explore the critical aspect of measuring TikTok marketing success. Effectively tracking and evaluating your performance on TikTok is essential for refining your strategy, achieving your objectives, and ensuring a positive return on investment (ROI).

Why Measuring TikTok Success Matters

Understanding the impact of your TikTok marketing efforts goes beyond vanity metrics like likes and followers. It provides valuable insights into your campaign's effectiveness, audience engagement, and overall performance. Here's why measuring TikTok success is crucial:

- **ROI Assessment**: Measuring success allows you to determine whether your TikTok campaigns are generating a positive return on your investment.
- **Strategy Refinement**: Data-driven insights help you refine your content strategy, optimizing for what works and discontinuing what doesn't.
- **Audience Understanding**: Analytics reveal important details about your audience's behaviour, preferences, and demographics, enabling you to tailor your content to their needs.
- **Goal Achievement**: Tracking progress toward specific

goals ensures that you're moving in the right direction and can adjust your strategy accordingly.

Key Metrics to Measure TikTok Success

Let's explore the essential metrics to measure TikTok marketing success:

1. Engagement Metrics

- **Likes**: The number of likes your videos receive is a basic indicator of audience approval.
- **Comments**: Comments reflect viewer engagement and may include questions, feedback, or user-generated content.
- **Shares**: The number of times viewers share your content with their followers indicates the viral potential of your videos.
- **Follows**: The number of new followers gained through your TikTok content reflects audience interest in your brand.

2. View Counts

- **Total Views**: The total number of times your videos have been viewed gives you an idea of your content's reach.
- **Average View Duration**: The average amount of time viewers spend watching your videos indicates their level of interest and engagement.

3. Click-Through Rate (CTR)

- CTR measures the percentage of viewers who click on a link or call-to-action (CTA) in your video or profile description.

4. Conversion Rate

- If your TikTok goal is to drive website traffic or sales, track the conversion rate—the percentage of viewers who complete the desired action.

5. Follower Growth

- Monitor your follower count over time to understand your TikTok account's growth rate.

6. Audience Demographics

- Analyse the demographics of your TikTok audience, including age, gender, location, and interests. This information helps you tailor your content.

7. Video Completion Rate

- Measure how many viewers watch your video until the end. A high completion rate indicates engaging content.

8. TikTok Analytics

- Utilize TikTok's built-in analytics tool, which provides detailed insights into video performance, audience demographics, and follower growth.

Best Practices for Measuring TikTok Success

Here are some best practices to effectively measure TikTok success:

1. Set Clear Goals: Define specific, measurable goals for your TikTok marketing campaigns. Whether it's increasing brand awareness, driving website traffic, or boosting sales, clear objectives are essential.

2. Use Analytics Tools: Leverage TikTok's analytics tools and third-party analytics platforms to gather comprehensive data about your performance.

3. Regularly Review Data: Establish a routine for reviewing your TikTok analytics data. Regular check-ins help you stay on top of trends and adapt your strategy as needed.

4. Compare Performance: Compare the performance of different videos to identify patterns and understand what resonates most with your audience.

5. Adjust Your Strategy: Based on your analytics insights, make informed adjustments to your content strategy, posting schedule, and targeting.

6. Test and Iterate: Continuously test new ideas, content formats, and CTAs to learn what works best for your audience.

Conclusion

Measuring TikTok marketing success is crucial for refining your strategy, optimizing your content, and achieving your marketing goals. By tracking key metrics and regularly analysing your performance, you can adapt and grow your presence on the platform effectively.

As you continue your TikTok marketing journey, remember that data-driven decision-making is essential for long-term success. In the upcoming chapters, we'll explore emerging trends and advanced strategies to keep you at the forefront of TikTok marketing.

CHAPTER 13: STAYING AHEAD WITH EMERGING TIKTOK TRENDS

Welcome to Chapter 13 of "TikTok Marketing Unveiled." In this chapter, we'll explore the importance of staying ahead with emerging TikTok trends. TikTok is a dynamic platform known for its rapidly evolving trends and challenges. As a business owner, being attuned to these trends can give you a competitive edge and enhance your marketing efforts.

Why Keep Up with TikTok Trends?

Staying up-to-date with emerging TikTok trends offers several benefits for your marketing strategy:

- **Relevance**: Embracing current trends shows that your brand is relevant and in touch with popular culture, making it more appealing to younger audiences.
- **Visibility**: Jumping on trending challenges or using trending sounds can increase the visibility of your content, potentially landing it on the "For You" page.
- **Engagement**: Participating in trends encourages viewer engagement through comments, likes, shares, and duets.
- **Creativity**: Trends can spark creativity and inspire fresh ideas for your TikTok content.

Tips for Identifying and Utilising Trends

Here are some tips for identifying and effectively utilising emerging TikTok trends:

1. Daily Exploration

- Dedicate time each day to explore TikTok trends and challenges. Browse through the "Discover" page and the "Trending" section to see what's popular.
- Follow creators who are known for participating in and starting trends.

2. Monitor Hashtags

- Keep an eye on trending hashtags. TikTok often promotes challenges and trends through specific hashtags, making them easy to find.
- Use these hashtags in your content to join the conversation.

3. Watch Your Competitors

- Observe what your competitors are doing on TikTok. Are they engaging in trends or creating unique content?
- Learn from their successes and incorporate similar strategies into your marketing efforts.

4. Be Authentic

- While participating in trends, maintain your brand's authenticity. Add your unique twist or style to stand out.
- Ensure that trend participation aligns with your brand's voice and values.

5. Act Quickly

- Many trends have a short lifespan on TikTok. Act quickly to leverage emerging trends while they're still popular.
- Timing is crucial to maximise your content's visibility and engagement.

6. Experiment and Innovate

- Don't limit yourself to just following trends. Experiment with your own creative ideas and concepts.
- Innovate and create content that has the potential to start a trend of its own.

7. Encourage User Participation

- Involve your audience in trend participation by creating challenges or contests related to your brand.
- Encourage viewers to create their own content around your challenges.

8. Stay Consistent

- Consistency in your content posting schedule is key to building a strong TikTok presence. Blend trend participation with your regular content strategy.

Conclusion

Staying ahead with emerging TikTok trends can breathe new life into your marketing strategy, enhance engagement, and boost your brand's visibility. However, it's important to participate in trends authentically and in a way that aligns with your brand's identity and values.

By keeping a watchful eye on trends, experimenting with creative ideas, and encouraging user participation, you can leverage TikTok's ever-evolving landscape to connect with your audience and stay ahead of the competition.

In the upcoming chapters, we'll explore additional advanced TikTok marketing strategies to help you further elevate your brand's presence on the platform.

CHAPTER 14: HARNESSING THE POWER OF TIKTOK CHALLENGES

Welcome to Chapter 14 of "TikTok Marketing Unveiled." In this chapter, we'll explore the world of TikTok challenges and how you can harness their power to enhance your marketing efforts. TikTok challenges are a popular and effective way to engage with your audience, increase brand awareness, and encourage user-generated content.

Understanding TikTok Challenges

TikTok challenges are viral trends that involve users creating and sharing videos based on a specific theme, concept, or hashtag. Challenges can be initiated by individuals, brands, or even TikTok itself. They are an exciting way to encourage user participation and creativity.

Here's why TikTok challenges are valuable for your marketing strategy:

- **User Engagement**: Challenges prompt users to actively participate, engage with your content, and create their own videos in response.
- **Viral Potential**: Successful challenges can go viral, reaching a wide audience and increasing brand visibility.

- **Community Building**: Challenges foster a sense of community as users come together to create and engage with content related to a common theme.

Creating and Promoting TikTok Challenges

Let's explore how to create and promote TikTok challenges effectively:

1. Define Your Goal

- Start by setting clear goals for your challenge. Do you want to increase brand awareness, drive user engagement, or promote a specific product or service?
- Ensure that your challenge aligns with your overall marketing objectives.

2. Conceptualise the Challenge

- Develop a creative and engaging challenge concept. Consider what will resonate with your target audience and how it can be expressed through short videos.
- Make the challenge easy to understand and participate in.

3. Choose a Hashtag

- Select a unique and catchy hashtag that encapsulates the essence of your challenge. The hashtag should be memorable and easy to spell.
- Promote the hashtag in all challenge-related content.

4. Create Engaging Content

- Launch the challenge with your own compelling TikTok video. This video should clearly explain the challenge, showcase your enthusiasm, and serve as an example for participants.
- Use music, effects, and visual elements to make your challenge video stand out.

5. Promote Across Platforms

- Promote your challenge on other social media platforms, your website, and email newsletters to reach a broader audience.
- Encourage your existing followers and customers to participate and spread the word.

6. Collaborate with Influencers

- Partner with TikTok influencers who align with your brand to help promote and participate in the challenge.
- Influencers can significantly increase the challenge's reach and engagement.

7. Engage and Share User Content

- Regularly engage with and share user-generated content related to your challenge. Recognize and celebrate participants by featuring their videos.
- Respond to comments and create a sense of community around the challenge.

8. Analyse and Adjust

- Use TikTok's analytics to track the performance of your challenge. Monitor metrics such as views, likes, shares, and user-generated content.
- Analyse the data to understand what worked well and what can be improved for future challenges.

9. Offer Prizes or Recognition

- Consider offering prizes or recognition to the best challenge participants. This can incentivise more users to join and create high-quality content.

10. Maintain Consistency

- Keep the momentum going by consistently promoting your challenge throughout its duration. Share updates, highlight participants, and encourage ongoing engagement.

Conclusion

TikTok challenges are a dynamic and effective way to engage with your audience, boost brand awareness, and encourage user-generated content. By setting clear goals, creating compelling content, and actively promoting your challenge, you can harness the power of TikTok challenges to enhance your marketing strategy.

As you continue to explore the world of TikTok marketing, remember that creativity and authenticity are key to creating challenges that resonate with your audience and achieve your marketing objectives. In the following chapters, we'll delve into additional advanced TikTok marketing strategies to further elevate your brand's presence on the platform.

CHAPTER 15: MASTERING TIKTOK ANALYTICS FOR SUCCESS

Welcome to Chapter 15 of "TikTok Marketing Unveiled." In this chapter, we'll dive deep into TikTok analytics and how you can use them to measure the effectiveness of your marketing efforts and make informed decisions to achieve success on the platform.

Why TikTok Analytics Matter

TikTok analytics provide invaluable insights into your TikTok account's performance, audience behaviour, and the impact of your content. Here's why TikTok analytics are essential:

- **Data-Driven Decision-Making**: Analytics empower you to make informed decisions by showing you which content is performing well and which areas need improvement.
- **Audience Understanding**: You can gain a better understanding of your audience's demographics, interests, and behaviour, helping you tailor your content to their preferences.
- **Goal Tracking**: Analytics allow you to track progress towards your specific marketing goals, whether it's increasing engagement, driving website traffic, or boosting sales.
- **Optimization**: With analytics, you can optimize your

content strategy, posting schedule, and ad campaigns for maximum impact.

Key TikTok Metrics to Monitor

Let's explore the key TikTok metrics you should monitor:

1. Follower Growth

- Track the growth of your follower count over time. This metric indicates how well your TikTok account is attracting and retaining followers.

2. Profile Views

- Monitor how many users visit your TikTok profile. A high number of profile views may indicate interest in your content.

3. Video Views

- Keep an eye on the total number of views your videos receive. This metric provides insights into the reach of your content.

4. Average Watch Time

- Measure the average amount of time viewers spend watching your videos. Longer watch times indicate that your content is engaging and retaining viewers' attention.

5. Likes, Comments, and Shares

- Analyse the number of likes, comments, and shares your videos receive. These metrics reflect audience engagement and interactions.

6. Audience Demographics

- TikTok provides data on your audience's demographics, including age, gender, location, and interests. Use this information to tailor your content.

7. Video Completion Rate

- Evaluate how many viewers watch your videos until the end. A high completion rate suggests that your content is captivating.

8. Engagement Rate

- Calculate the engagement rate by dividing the total number of likes, comments, and shares by the total number of video views. This metric provides a more comprehensive view of audience interaction.

9. Click-Through Rate (CTR)

- If you include links or call-to-actions (CTAs) in your videos or profile, track the CTR to measure how many viewers click through to your website or other destinations.

10. Conversion Rate

- If your goal is to drive conversions, such as product purchases or sign-ups, monitor the conversion rate—the percentage of viewers who complete the desired action.

Using TikTok Analytics Effectively

Here's how to use TikTok analytics effectively to enhance your marketing strategy:

1. Set Clear Objectives

- Start by defining clear and measurable goals for your TikTok marketing efforts. Your objectives will guide the metrics you prioritise.

2. Regularly Review Data

- Establish a routine for reviewing your TikTok analytics data. Regular check-ins help you identify trends and areas for improvement.

3. Compare Performance

- Compare the performance of different videos to identify patterns and understand what resonates most with your audience.

4. Experiment and Iterate

- Use insights from your analytics to experiment with different content types, posting schedules, and strategies. Continuously refine your approach based on data.

5. Adjust Your Content Strategy

- Tailor your content strategy to align with the preferences and behaviours of your TikTok audience. Create content that caters to their interests.

6. Track ROI

- If your goal is to generate revenue, closely monitor the ROI of your TikTok marketing campaigns. Assess whether your efforts are resulting in a positive return on investment.

7. Stay Updated

- TikTok frequently updates its analytics features. Stay informed about these changes to take full advantage of the platform's analytics capabilities.

Conclusion

Mastering TikTok analytics is essential for achieving success on the platform. By regularly monitoring key metrics, setting clear objectives, and making data-driven decisions, you can optimize your TikTok marketing strategy, engage your audience effectively, and work towards your marketing goals.

In the upcoming chapters, we'll explore advanced TikTok marketing strategies and trends to help you stay at the forefront of TikTok marketing.

CHAPTER 16: BUILDING TIKTOK COMMUNITIES AND FOSTERING ENGAGEMENT

Welcome to Chapter 16 of "TikTok Marketing Unveiled." In this chapter, we'll delve into the art of building TikTok communities and fostering engagement among your followers. Building a strong community on TikTok is essential for long-term success, brand loyalty, and sustained growth.

The Value of TikTok Communities

TikTok communities are groups of like-minded users who share common interests, passions, or challenges. Nurturing a TikTok community around your brand or content can yield several benefits:

- **Loyal Audience**: A dedicated community is more likely to engage with your content consistently and become loyal followers.
- **User-Generated Content**: Communities often generate user-generated content (UGC) related to your brand or challenges, further expanding your reach.
- **Feedback and Insights**: Engaged communities provide valuable feedback and insights, helping you refine your

content and offerings.

- **Advocacy**: Community members can become brand advocates, promoting your content and products to their followers.

Strategies for Building TikTok Communities

Let's explore strategies for building and nurturing TikTok communities:

1. Identify Your Niche

- Determine your niche and target audience. Understanding your audience's interests and preferences is the first step in building a community.

2. Consistent Content

- Consistency is key. Post high-quality content regularly to keep your audience engaged and returning for more.

3. Engage Actively

- Respond to comments, engage with followers through duets and collaborations, and actively participate in trending challenges.

4. Create Challenges

- Launch your unique challenges to encourage user participation. Create a dedicated hashtag for your challenge to track submissions.

5. Encourage User-Generated Content

- Feature user-generated content related to your brand, products, or challenges in your videos. Recognise and celebrate your community's contributions.

6. Live Streams and Q&A Sessions

- Host live streams to interact with your audience in real-time. Answer questions, share insights, and create a sense of community.

7. Collaborate with Influencers

- Partner with TikTok influencers who share your niche. Their engagement can introduce your brand to their followers and expand your community.

8. Reward Engagement

- Organise giveaways, contests, or exclusive perks for your community members who actively engage with your content.

9. Share Behind-the-Scenes Content

- Show the human side of your brand by sharing behind-the-scenes glimpses, day-in-the-life videos, and personal anecdotes.

10. Listen and Adapt

- Pay attention to your community's feedback. Listen to their suggestions and adapt your content and strategies accordingly.

Measuring Community Engagement

Measuring community engagement is essential to assess the health of your TikTok community. Key metrics include:

- **Comments**: The number and quality of comments on your videos.
- **Shares**: How frequently your content is shared by your community members.
- **Follower Growth**: Tracking how your community is growing over time.
- **Participation in Challenges**: The number of users participating in your challenges.
- **User-Generated Content**: The volume of content generated by your community in response to your challenges or prompts.

Conclusion

Building TikTok communities and fostering engagement is an ongoing process that requires dedication and authenticity. By creating valuable content, actively engaging with your followers, and encouraging user participation, you can cultivate a vibrant TikTok community around your brand or content.

Remember that nurturing a community takes time and effort, but the rewards in terms of brand loyalty and sustained growth are well worth it. In the upcoming chapters, we'll continue to explore advanced TikTok marketing strategies and trends to help you further enhance your brand's presence on the platform.

CHAPTER 17: LEVERAGING TIKTOK ADS FOR BUSINESS GROWTH

Welcome to Chapter 17 of "TikTok Marketing Unveiled." In this chapter, we'll explore the powerful world of TikTok ads and how you can leverage them to drive business growth. TikTok offers a range of advertising options to help businesses reach a broader audience, increase brand awareness, and achieve their marketing objectives.

Why Advertise on TikTok?

TikTok has rapidly become a global social media powerhouse with a massive user base, making it an attractive platform for businesses. Here are some compelling reasons to advertise on TikTok:

- **Wide Audience Reach**: TikTok boasts a diverse and engaged user base, providing businesses with an opportunity to reach a broad demographic.
- **Creative Freedom**: TikTok's creative and visually appealing format allows businesses to showcase their products or services in innovative ways.
- **Effective Targeting**: TikTok offers advanced targeting options based on demographics, interests, behaviour, and more, ensuring that your ads reach the right audience.

- **High Engagement**: TikTok users are known for their high engagement levels, making it easier for businesses to capture viewers' attention.

Types of TikTok Ads

Let's explore the primary types of TikTok ads available to businesses:

- **In-Feed Ads**: These are short video ads that appear in users' "For You" feed as they scroll through TikTok. They can be up to 60 seconds long and include a clickable link.
- **Branded Hashtag Challenges**: Brands create unique challenges, encourage user participation, and promote them using a sponsored hashtag. This can lead to viral engagement.
- **Branded Effects**: Brands can create customised augmented reality (AR) effects and filters for users to use in their videos. These effects promote brand recognition.
- **TopView Ads**: These are in-feed ads but have the added benefit of being the first thing users see when they open the TikTok app. They offer maximum visibility.
- **Branded Content**: Collaborate with popular TikTok creators to promote your products or services authentically. Creators can produce engaging content that resonates with their followers.

Creating Effective TikTok Ads

Here's how to create effective TikTok ads for your business:

- **Define Your Goals**: Clearly define your advertising goals, whether it's brand awareness, website traffic, or sales conversions.
- **Audience Targeting**: Utilize TikTok's advanced

targeting options to reach the most relevant audience for your campaign.

- **Compelling Creative**: Create visually appealing, engaging, and concise ad content that aligns with your brand's messaging.
- **Clear Call-to-Action**: Include a clear call-to-action (CTA) in your ad to prompt viewers to take the desired action, such as clicking a link or making a purchase.
- **Testing and Optimization**: Continuously test different ad creatives and optimise your campaigns based on performance data.
- **Budget Management**: Set a reasonable budget for your ad campaign and allocate resources effectively.
- **Track and Measure**: Monitor the performance of your TikTok ads using the platform's analytics. Track key metrics such as click-through rate (CTR), conversion rate, and return on ad spend (ROAS).

Benefits of TikTok Ads

Advertising on TikTok offers several benefits for businesses:

- **Increased Visibility**: TikTok ads can significantly increase brand visibility and reach, especially when used in conjunction with popular challenges or trends.
- **Lead Generation**: TikTok ads can help generate leads and drive website traffic, allowing businesses to capture potential customers.
- **Audience Engagement**: Engaging ad content can foster a deeper connection with your target audience and encourage them to interact with your brand.
- **Brand Awareness**: TikTok ads are an effective way to build and reinforce brand awareness among a wide audience.

Conclusion

Leveraging TikTok ads for business growth can be a game-changer in your marketing strategy. With its diverse user base, creative potential, and effective targeting options, TikTok offers a unique platform for businesses to expand their reach and achieve their marketing goals.

As you venture into TikTok advertising, remember to define clear objectives, create compelling content, and regularly analyse your ad campaign's performance to ensure a positive return on investment (ROI). In the upcoming chapters, we'll continue to explore advanced TikTok marketing strategies to help you further enhance your brand's presence on the platform.

CHAPTER 18: TIKTOK INFLUENCER MARKETING STRATEGIES

Welcome to Chapter 18 of "TikTok Marketing Unveiled." In this chapter, we'll explore the world of TikTok influencer marketing and how you can leverage influencers to enhance your brand's presence, engage your target audience, and achieve your marketing goals on the platform.

The Power of TikTok Influencer Marketing

Influencer marketing on TikTok has gained tremendous popularity due to the platform's large and engaged user base. TikTok influencers have the ability to connect with their followers authentically and can significantly amplify your brand's reach and impact. Here's why TikTok influencer marketing matters:

- **Authenticity**: Influencers are seen as trustworthy sources by their followers, making their endorsements more authentic and effective.
- **Wider Reach**: TikTok influencers have substantial followings, allowing your brand to reach a larger and more targeted audience.
- **Engagement**: Influencers can create engaging and relatable content that resonates with their followers, resulting in higher engagement rates.
- **Creativity**: TikTok influencers are known for their

creative content, which can help your brand stand out and capture viewers' attention.

Effective TikTok Influencer Marketing Strategies

To harness the power of TikTok influencer marketing effectively, consider these strategies:

1. Identify the Right Influencers

- Look for influencers whose values, interests, and audience align with your brand. The right fit is crucial for authenticity.
- Check an influencer's engagement rate, audience demographics, and past collaborations to assess their effectiveness.

2. Define Clear Objectives

- Clearly define your influencer marketing objectives, whether it's increasing brand awareness, driving sales, or launching a new product.
- Communicate your goals and expectations clearly to the influencer.

3. Collaborate on Content

- Work closely with the influencer to create content that aligns with your brand's message and campaign objectives.
- Allow influencers creative freedom to ensure authenticity in their content.

4. Leverage Challenges and Trends

- Encourage influencers to participate in or create challenges and trends related to your brand. This can boost engagement and user-generated content.

5. Transparent Partnerships

- Ensure that influencer partnerships are transparent and disclose sponsored content appropriately, as per

TikTok's guidelines.

6. Track and Measure Performance

- Monitor the performance of influencer campaigns using TikTok's analytics and track key metrics such as engagement, reach, and conversions.

7. Foster Long-Term Relationships

- Building long-term relationships with influencers can be more beneficial than one-off collaborations. It allows for consistent brand representation and audience connection.

8. Micro-Influencers

- Consider working with micro-influencers (influencers with smaller but highly engaged followings) to reach niche audiences effectively.

9. Offer Value

- Provide influencers with value beyond monetary compensation, such as access to exclusive products, early releases, or unique experiences.

10. Authenticity is Key

- Encourage influencers to authentically integrate your brand into their content rather than appearing overly promotional.

Measuring the Success of Influencer Campaigns

To gauge the success of your TikTok influencer campaigns, consider the following metrics:

- **Engagement Rate**: Measure the likes, comments, shares, and views generated by the influencer's content.
- **Follower Growth**: Track how many new followers your brand gains as a result of the influencer collaboration.
- **Conversion Rate**: If the goal is to drive sales or website traffic, monitor the conversion rate—the percentage of viewers who complete the desired action.
- **Reach and Impressions**: Evaluate the overall reach and impressions of the influencer's content.
- **Audience Demographics**: Understand the demographics of the audience reached through the influencer campaign.

Conclusion

TikTok influencer marketing is a powerful strategy for businesses looking to connect with a larger and engaged audience. By identifying the right influencers, setting clear objectives, collaborating on creative content, and measuring performance effectively, you can harness the authenticity and reach of influencers to achieve your marketing goals on TikTok.

As you venture into influencer marketing, remember that authenticity and a genuine connection between the influencer and your brand are paramount for success. In the following chapters, we'll explore additional advanced TikTok marketing strategies and trends to further elevate your brand's presence on the platform.

CHAPTER 19: GOING VIRAL ON TIKTOK: STRATEGIES FOR SUCCESS

Welcome to Chapter 19 of "TikTok Marketing Unveiled." In this chapter, we'll explore the elusive and highly coveted concept of going viral on TikTok. Going viral can dramatically boost your brand's visibility, engage a massive audience, and propel your marketing efforts to new heights.

Understanding TikTok Virality

TikTok is known for its viral content—videos that rapidly gain millions of views, likes, and shares. Virality on TikTok often happens when your content resonates with a broad audience, sparking curiosity, emotion, or participation. Here's why it matters:

- **Exponential Reach**: Viral content can reach an exponentially larger audience than regular posts, increasing brand exposure.
- **Engagement**: Viral videos typically generate high levels of engagement, with viewers liking, sharing, and commenting.
- **Brand Awareness**: Going viral can significantly boost brand awareness, making your brand more memorable among users.

Strategies for Going Viral on TikTok

While there's no guaranteed formula for virality, several strategies can increase your chances of going viral on TikTok:

1. Create High-Quality Content

- Invest in high-quality video production. Clear audio, sharp visuals, and creative editing can make your content more appealing.

2. Embrace Trends and Challenges

- Participate in popular challenges and trends. Use trending sounds, hashtags, and effects to increase the discoverability of your content.

3. Storytelling

- Craft compelling and relatable stories that captivate viewers emotionally. Personal narratives often resonate strongly.

4. Hook Viewers Early

- Capture viewers' attention within the first few seconds of your video. The opening is crucial for retention and sharing.

5. Surprise and Delight

- Surprise your audience with unexpected twists, humour, or creativity. A pleasant surprise can encourage sharing.

6. Engage Emotions

- Create content that elicits strong emotions, whether it's laughter, awe, empathy, or inspiration. Emotional content tends to go viral.

7. User-Generated Content

- Encourage user-generated content related to your brand or challenges. The more users participate, the wider your reach.

8. Collaborate

- Collaborate with other TikTok creators, especially those with a large following. Their audience may discover and engage with your content.

9. Consistency

- Post regularly to keep your audience engaged and increase the chances of one of your videos going viral.

10. Experiment

- Don't be afraid to try different content formats, styles, and approaches. What worked once may not work every time.

11. Engage with Your Audience

- Respond to comments and engage with your viewers. A strong connection can lead to more sharing and interaction.

12. Leverage Timing

- Pay attention to current events, holidays, and trends. Timely content can capture attention and go viral.

13. Cross-Promote

- Share your TikTok videos on other social media platforms to reach a wider audience and potentially go viral on multiple platforms.

Measuring Virality

While the definition of viral can vary, some key metrics can indicate the virality of your TikTok content:

- **Views**: A high number of views in a short time is a

strong indicator of potential virality.

- **Shares**: Monitor how many times your video has been shared. Sharing often signals that viewers find the content share-worthy.
- **Comments**: Viral videos tend to generate a substantial number of comments as viewers engage in discussions.
- **Likes**: A high number of likes can signify that viewers enjoyed and appreciated your content.
- **Follower Growth**: Viral videos often result in a significant increase in followers.

Conclusion

Going viral on TikTok is a thrilling experience that can catapult your brand's visibility and engagement to unprecedented levels. While there's no guaranteed path to virality, creating high-quality, emotionally engaging, and trendy content, coupled with audience interaction and collaboration, can significantly increase your chances.

As you strive for virality, remember that authenticity and a deep understanding of your target audience are crucial. In the upcoming chapters, we'll explore advanced TikTok marketing strategies and trends to help you further enhance your brand's presence on the platform.

CHAPTER 20: MEASURING TIKTOK ROI AND SCALING SUCCESS

Welcome to Chapter 20 of "TikTok Marketing Unveiled." In this chapter, we'll explore the critical aspects of measuring Return on Investment (ROI) on TikTok and how to scale your success on the platform. Understanding your TikTok marketing ROI is essential for assessing the effectiveness of your efforts and making informed decisions for future campaigns.

Why Measuring TikTok ROI Matters

Measuring TikTok ROI allows you to:

- **Assess Campaign Effectiveness**: Determine which TikTok campaigns are generating the best results, whether it's increased brand awareness, website traffic, or sales.
- **Allocate Resources Wisely**: Make informed decisions about where to allocate your marketing budget for maximum impact.
- **Demonstrate Value**: Provide stakeholders with evidence of the value and impact of your TikTok marketing efforts.

Measuring TikTok ROI

Here's how to measure TikTok ROI effectively:

1. Set Clear Goals

- Start by defining clear and measurable goals for your TikTok marketing campaigns. These goals will be the basis for measuring ROI.

2. Calculate Investment

- Determine the total investment in your TikTok marketing, including ad spend, influencer fees, content production costs, and any other expenses.

3. Track Key Metrics

- Utilise TikTok's analytics and tracking tools to monitor key performance indicators (KPIs) relevant to your goals. These may include views, engagement, click-through rates (CTR), conversion rates, and revenue generated.

4. Calculate ROI

- Calculate ROI using the following formula:
- ROI = (Net Profit - Investment) / Investment * 100
  - Net Profit includes the revenue generated from your TikTok marketing efforts minus the costs associated with those efforts.

5. Attribution Models

- Consider the attribution model that best suits your marketing goals. Single-touch attribution models credit a single touchpoint (e.g., first click or last click), while multi-touch models assign value to multiple interactions along the customer journey.

6. Benchmark Performance

- Compare the ROI of your TikTok marketing campaigns to industry benchmarks and your own historical data. This provides context for your results.

Scaling Success on TikTok

After measuring ROI, the next step is to scale your success on TikTok. Here are strategies to help you achieve this:

1. Invest Strategically

- Allocate more budget to the TikTok campaigns and strategies that have proven to deliver a positive ROI. Focus on what works.

2. Expand Your Reach

- Consider increasing your reach by collaborating with more influencers, running additional ads, and exploring new content formats.

3. Experiment and Innovate

- Continue to experiment with new content ideas, ad formats, and trends. Staying fresh and innovative can help you maintain success.

4. Optimise Ad Spend

- Regularly review and optimize your ad campaigns to ensure you're getting the most value for your budget. Adjust targeting, bidding, and creative elements as needed.

5. Audience Segmentation

- Segment your TikTok audience based on their behaviour, demographics, and interests. Tailor content and campaigns to specific segments for better results.

6. Analyse Data

- Continue to monitor and analyse TikTok analytics to identify trends, patterns, and areas for improvement.

7. Leverage User-Generated Content

- Encourage your audience to create and share user-generated content related to your brand or challenges. This can amplify your reach and engagement.

8. Long-Term Relationships

- Nurture long-term relationships with TikTok influencers who align with your brand. Consistent collaborations can lead to sustained success.

Conclusion

Measuring TikTok ROI and scaling success are integral parts of your TikTok marketing journey. By setting clear goals, tracking key metrics, calculating ROI, and making data-driven decisions, you can not only evaluate the effectiveness of your TikTok marketing efforts but also optimize and expand them to achieve even greater success on the platform.

Remember that TikTok marketing is dynamic, and staying adaptable and responsive to changes in audience behaviour and platform features is key to continued success. With these strategies in mind, you can continue to elevate your brand's presence on TikTok and contribute to its growth and success.

CHAPTER 21: STAYING AHEAD WITH EMERGING TIKTOK TRENDS

Welcome to Chapter 21 of "TikTok Marketing Unveiled." In this chapter, we'll explore the importance of staying ahead with emerging TikTok trends to maintain relevance, engage your audience, and continually elevate your brand's presence on the platform. TikTok is a dynamic and ever-evolving platform, and staying current with trends is essential for TikTok marketing success.

The Significance of TikTok Trends

TikTok trends play a pivotal role in shaping the content landscape on the platform. Here's why they matter:

- **User Engagement**: Participating in trending challenges and using popular sounds can boost user engagement and visibility.
- **Discoverability**: Trending content is often prominently featured on TikTok's discovery page, making it more accessible to a wider audience.
- **Relevance**: Staying current with trends shows that your brand is active and relevant on TikTok, which can help maintain user interest.

Strategies for Embracing TikTok Trends

Here are strategies to help you embrace TikTok trends effectively:

1. Active Observation

- Regularly browse TikTok to observe and identify emerging trends, challenges, and popular sounds. Pay attention to what's resonating with the audience.

2. Strategic Participation

- Participate in trending challenges that align with your brand's values and message. Ensure your content feels natural and relevant within the context of the trend.

3. Creative Interpretation

- Put a unique and creative spin on trends to make your content stand out. Originality can capture viewers' attention.

4. Collaborations

- Collaborate with TikTok influencers or other content creators who are known for participating in and starting trends. Their involvement can boost your campaign's visibility.

5. Trend-Related Hashtags

- Use trending hashtags associated with popular challenges to increase the discoverability of your content.

6. Consistency

- Regularly participate in trending challenges and incorporate trending sounds into your content. Consistency can help you maintain relevance.

7. Trend Forecasting

- Keep an eye on social media and industry news for trend forecasts and predictions. Staying ahead of the curve can give you a competitive advantage.

8. Data Analysis

- Analyse TikTok analytics to track the performance of your trend-related content. Understand which trends resonate most with your audience.

9. User Feedback

- Listen to feedback from your TikTok audience. Engage with comments and consider suggestions for future content.

10. Content Calendar

- Develop a content calendar that incorporates planned participation in trending challenges and trends. This can help you stay organized and prepared.

TikTok Trend Categories

TikTok trends can encompass a wide range of categories, including:

- **Dance Challenges**: Choreographed dances to popular songs.
- **Comedy Skits**: Short and humorous sketches.
- **Lip Syncing**: Syncing your lips to songs, dialogues, or voiceovers.

- **Educational Trends**: Informative and instructional content.
- **Cooking and Food Trends**: Sharing cooking tips, recipes, and food-related content.
- **DIY and Hacks**: Demonstrating do-it-yourself projects and life hacks.
- **Beauty and Fashion Trends**: Showcasing makeup, fashion, and styling tips.
- **Pet and Animal Trends**: Featuring cute or funny pet videos.
- **Challenge and Dare Trends**: Encouraging viewers to complete challenges or dares.
- **Cultural Trends**: Celebrating cultural events, traditions, and heritage.

Conclusion

Staying ahead with emerging TikTok trends is an integral part of maintaining a vibrant and relevant presence on the platform. By actively observing, strategically participating, and creatively interpreting trends, you can engage your audience, boost discoverability, and keep your brand at the forefront of TikTok's dynamic content landscape.

Remember that TikTok trends can evolve quickly, so adaptability and a willingness to experiment are key to success. As you continue your TikTok marketing journey, staying attuned to emerging trends will help you stay current and continually elevate your brand's TikTok presence.

CHAPTER 22: TIKTOK'S EVOLVING LANDSCAPE: WHAT THE FUTURE HOLDS

Welcome to Chapter 22 of "TikTok Marketing Unveiled." In this chapter, we'll explore the ever-evolving landscape of TikTok and what the future may hold for the platform. Staying informed about TikTok's trajectory is essential for businesses looking to maintain a successful TikTok marketing strategy.

TikTok's Remarkable Growth

TikTok's growth has been nothing short of remarkable. It has become a global social media phenomenon, with billions of users worldwide. However, the social media landscape is dynamic, and platforms continuously evolve. Here are some key factors to consider:

1. Expanding User Base

- TikTok is likely to continue expanding its user base, especially in markets where it is still gaining traction. New demographics and regions may present opportunities for businesses.

2. Enhanced Advertising Tools

- TikTok is expected to further refine and expand its advertising offerings. This includes improved targeting options, ad formats, and analytics for businesses to leverage.

3. Algorithm Refinements

- TikTok's algorithm, which drives content discovery, will likely undergo refinements to provide users with even more personalised content. Businesses should stay adaptable to these changes.

4. Regulatory Challenges

- TikTok has faced regulatory scrutiny in some countries. Staying informed about regulatory changes and how they may impact your TikTok marketing is crucial.

5. Competition

- Competition in the social media space is fierce. Keep an eye on emerging platforms and trends that may influence user behaviour and content consumption.

Strategies for Navigating TikTok's Future

To navigate TikTok's evolving landscape successfully, consider these strategies:

1. Stay Informed

- Continuously monitor TikTok news, updates, and announcements. TikTok often introduces new features and changes, so staying informed is essential.

2. Adaptability

- Be prepared to adapt your TikTok marketing strategy in response to platform changes, audience shifts, and emerging trends.

3. Diversification

- Explore opportunities to diversify your social media

presence. While TikTok may be a valuable platform, consider maintaining a presence on other relevant platforms as well.

4. User-First Approach

- Keep your audience's preferences and behaviour at the forefront of your strategy. Create content that resonates with your target audience.

5. Creative Innovation

- Continue to innovate and experiment with content formats, trends, and ad strategies to stay relevant and engage your audience.

6. Cross-Platform Integration

- Consider integrating your TikTok marketing efforts with other marketing channels for a cohesive brand presence.

7. Data-Driven Decisions

- Base your decisions on data and analytics. Regularly assess the performance of your TikTok marketing campaigns to make informed choices.

8. Authenticity

- Authenticity remains a cornerstone of effective TikTok marketing. Ensure that your brand's message and content align with your values and resonate with your audience.

Conclusion

The future of TikTok promises exciting opportunities and challenges for businesses. By staying informed, adaptable, and committed to creating engaging and authentic content, you can navigate TikTok's evolving landscape successfully and continue to leverage the platform to achieve your marketing goals.

Remember that TikTok's success is driven by its dynamic and engaged user base. As long as you remain attentive to your audience's preferences and responsive to changes, TikTok can remain a valuable platform for your brand's marketing endeavours.

CHAPTER 23:
TIKTOK MARKETING
CASE STUDIES

Welcome to Chapter 23 of "TikTok Marketing Unveiled." In this chapter, we'll delve into real-world TikTok marketing case studies to provide you with practical insights and inspiration for your own TikTok marketing campaigns. These success stories showcase how businesses have effectively leveraged TikTok to achieve their marketing objectives.

Case Study 1: e.l.f. Cosmetics

Objective: e.l.f. Cosmetics, a cosmetics brand, aimed to increase brand awareness and engagement among a younger demographic.

Strategy:

- e.l.f. Cosmetics launched the #eyeslipsface challenge, encouraging users to showcase their makeup transformation using e.l.f. products.
- The challenge featured a catchy song and creative makeup transitions, making it highly shareable.

Results:

- The #eyeslipsface challenge went viral, generating over 6 billion views and inspiring millions of user-generated videos.
- e.l.f. Cosmetics gained a massive increase in brand visibility and engagement among TikTok's younger user

base.

Key Takeaway: Leveraging TikTok challenges with catchy music and engaging content can lead to viral success.

Case Study 2: Chipotle Mexican Grill

Objective: Chipotle aimed to promote its delivery service and engage TikTok's younger audience.

Strategy:

- Chipotle partnered with TikTok influencer David Dobrik for the #ChipotleLidFlip challenge.
- The challenge involved flipping Chipotle's iconic lids onto their burrito bowls in creative ways.

Results:

- The #ChipotleLidFlip challenge generated over 110,000 user-generated videos and 104 million video views in just six days.
- Chipotle's partnership with David Dobrik resulted in significant brand exposure and increased awareness of their delivery service.

Key Takeaway: Collaborating with popular TikTok influencers can amplify your campaign's reach and impact.

Case Study 3: Ocean Spray

Objective: Ocean Spray aimed to revitalise its brand image and appeal to a younger audience.

Strategy:

- The "Dreams" challenge was born when TikTok user @420doggface208 posted a video of himself skateboarding while drinking Ocean Spray cranberry juice and listening to Fleetwood Mac's "Dreams."
- Ocean Spray embraced the challenge, sending a cranberry juice supply to @420doggface208 and launching the #DreamsChallenge.

Results:

- The #DreamsChallenge became a cultural phenomenon, with countless users recreating the iconic skateboard video.
- Ocean Spray experienced a surge in positive brand sentiment, reaching a younger demographic and revitalizing its image.

Key Takeaway: Embracing user-generated content and trends can lead to unexpected and highly successful marketing campaigns.

Conclusion

These TikTok marketing case studies illustrate the diverse ways in which brands have harnessed the platform's creative potential, viral challenges, and influencer partnerships to achieve their marketing goals. Whether it's increasing brand awareness, engaging a younger audience, or revitalizing brand image, TikTok offers a unique platform for innovative and effective marketing strategies.

As you consider your own TikTok marketing campaigns, draw inspiration from these case studies and adapt the strategies to suit your brand's objectives and audience. Remember that TikTok's dynamic and creative nature provides ample opportunities for businesses to make a meaningful impact on the platform.

CHAPTER 24: TIKTOK MARKETING BEST PRACTICES

Welcome to Chapter 24 of "TikTok Marketing Unveiled." In this chapter, we'll cover a comprehensive set of best practices to help you maximise the effectiveness of your TikTok marketing efforts. Whether you're a beginner or an experienced TikTok marketer, these practices will guide you in creating compelling content and achieving your marketing objectives on the platform.

1. Understand Your Audience

- Before creating content, thoroughly understand your target audience's preferences, interests, and behaviour on TikTok. Tailor your content to resonate with them.

2. Consistent Branding

- Maintain consistent branding across your TikTok profile, including profile picture, username, and bio. This helps users recognise and remember your brand.

3. Creative Storytelling

- Engage your audience through storytelling. Craft narratives that captivate and emotionally connect with viewers.

4. Keep It Short and Sweet

- TikTok thrives on short-form video content. Keep your videos concise, typically under 60 seconds, to maintain viewer engagement.

5. High-Quality Production

- Invest in good video and audio quality. Clear visuals and sound enhance the overall viewer experience.

6. Utilise Trending Sounds and Hashtags

- Incorporate trending sounds and relevant hashtags in your content to increase discoverability and engagement.

7. Authenticity is Key

- Be authentic in your content. TikTok users appreciate genuine and relatable content.

8. Engage with Your Audience

- Respond to comments and engage with your audience. Building a community fosters a deeper connection.

9. Collaborate with Influencers

- Collaborate with TikTok influencers who align with your brand. Influencers can help you reach a wider and more engaged audience.

10. Test and Learn

- Experiment with different content formats, styles, and strategies. Analyse what works best for your brand and audience.

11. Use Captivating Thumbnails

- Choose engaging video thumbnails to entice viewers to click and watch your content.

12. Create Educational Content

- Share valuable insights, tips, and educational content related to your industry or niche. Position your brand as a knowledgeable resource.

13. Encourage User Participation

- Design challenges and campaigns that encourage user participation. User-generated content can amplify your brand's reach.

14. Optimise Your Bio

- Write a concise and engaging bio that communicates your brand's identity and purpose.

15. Test Posting Times

- Experiment with different posting times to determine when your audience is most active and responsive.

16. Monitor TikTok Analytics

- Regularly review TikTok's analytics to track your performance, audience demographics, and video engagement.

17. Cross-Promotion

- Promote your TikTok content on other social media platforms to drive traffic and engagement.

18. Safety and Community Guidelines

- Adhere to TikTok's safety and community guidelines to ensure your content complies with the platform's policies.

19. Stay Current

- Stay informed about TikTok trends, features, and updates. TikTok's landscape evolves rapidly.

20. Consistency

- Maintain a consistent posting schedule to keep your audience engaged and returning for more content.

21. Measure ROI

- Regularly measure the return on investment (ROI) of your TikTok marketing campaigns to assess their effectiveness.

Conclusion

These TikTok marketing best practices serve as a roadmap to help you navigate the dynamic and creative world of TikTok. By implementing these strategies, you can create compelling content, engage your target audience, and achieve your marketing objectives on the platform. Remember that TikTok offers a unique and ever-evolving space for businesses to connect with their audience and stand out in the digital landscape.

CHAPTER 25: TIKTOK MARKETING CONCLUSION AND YOUR JOURNEY AHEAD

Congratulations on completing "TikTok Marketing Unveiled!" In this final chapter, we'll wrap up your TikTok marketing journey and provide you with key takeaways, actionable steps, and a glimpse into what lies ahead in your marketing endeavours on TikTok.

Key Takeaways from Your TikTok Marketing Journey

- **Authenticity Matters:** TikTok thrives on authentic, relatable content. Be genuine in your brand's messaging and interactions with the TikTok community.
- **Stay Current:** TikTok is ever-evolving. Stay informed about the latest trends, features, and updates to maintain relevance.
- **Engage Your Audience:** Building a community on TikTok is crucial. Engage with your audience through comments, likes, and responses.
- **Creativity Wins:** TikTok rewards creativity. Don't be afraid to experiment with content formats, trends, and challenges.
- **Collaboration is Powerful:** Partnering with influencers

and collaborating with other TikTok creators can amplify your brand's reach and impact.

- **Measure ROI:** Regularly assess the return on investment (ROI) of your TikTok marketing campaigns to make informed decisions.

Your Next Steps on TikTok

As you continue your TikTok marketing journey, consider the following steps:

- **Set Clear Objectives:** Define your marketing goals on TikTok. Whether it's brand awareness, engagement, website traffic or sales, clarity is essential.
- **Content Planning:** Create a content calendar that aligns with your objectives and includes a mix of trends, challenges, and original content.
- **Influencer Collaborations:** Explore influencer partnerships that align with your brand. Collaborations can significantly boost your reach.
- **Analytics Insights:** Regularly analyse TikTok analytics to understand your audience, track performance, and adjust your strategy accordingly.
- **Consistency is Key:** Maintain a consistent posting schedule to keep your audience engaged and returning for more content.
- **Stay Adaptable:** TikTok is dynamic, and what works today may not work tomorrow. Stay adaptable and open to change.
- **Diversify Your Content:** Experiment with various content formats, from short skits to educational videos, to cater to different audience preferences.

The Future of TikTok Marketing

TikTok's future holds exciting possibilities for businesses. The platform is likely to continue evolving, offering new opportunities for creative marketing strategies. Here are some potential trends:

- **E-commerce Integration:** TikTok may further integrate e-commerce features, making it easier for businesses to sell products directly on the platform.
- **Augmented Reality (AR):** AR filters and effects could become more sophisticated, providing innovative marketing opportunities.
- **Interactive Content:** Interactive elements, like polls and quizzes, may gain prominence for user engagement.
- **Data-Driven Insights:** TikTok's analytics tools may become more robust, allowing for deeper insights and more effective targeting.
- **Emerging Trends:** Keep an eye on emerging trends and adapt your strategy to incorporate them for maximum impact.

Your Journey Continues

Your journey in TikTok marketing doesn't end here. TikTok's dynamic nature ensures that there will always be new opportunities and challenges to explore. As you continue your TikTok marketing efforts, remember that authenticity, creativity, and a deep understanding of your audience will be your greatest assets.

Thank you for joining us on this TikTok marketing adventure. We wish you success, creativity, and boundless opportunities as you continue to grow your brand's presence and engage with the vibrant TikTok community.

Keep **TikToking!**

Dan J. Fordham